NAVIGATING
ISAIAH
WITH BYRON THOMAS

Abingdon Press | Nashville

NAVIGATING ISAIAH

Copyright© 2021 Abingdon Press
All rights reserved.

No part of this work may be reproduced or transmitted in any form or by any means, electronic or mechanical, including photocopying and recording, or by any information or retrieval system, except as may be expressly permitted in the 1976 Copyright Act or in writing from the publisher. Requests for permission should be addressed in writing to Permissions, The United Methodist Publishing House, 2222 Rosa L. Parks Blvd., Nashville, TN 37228-0988 or e-mailed to permissions@umpublishing.org.

ISBN 978-1-7910-2367-6

All Scripture quotations, unless otherwise indicated, are taken from the Holy Bible, New International Version®, NIV®. Copyright ©1973, 1978, 1984, 2011 by Biblica, Inc.™ Used by permission of Zondervan. All rights reserved worldwide. www.zondervan.com The "NIV" and "New International Version" are trademarks registered in the United States Patent and Trademark Office by Biblica, Inc.™

Scripture quotations marked (CEV) are from the Contemporary English Version Copyright © 1991, 1992, 1995 by American Bible Society, Used by Permission.

Scripture quotations marked (NRSV) are taken from the New Revised Standard Version of the Bible, copyright 1989, Division of Christian Education of the National Council of the Churches of Christ in the United States of America. Used by permission. All rights reserved.

Manufactured in the United States of America
21 22 23 24 25 26 27 28 29 30—10 9 8 7 6 5 4 3 2 1

CONTENTS

Introduction 5

1. Prophecies Against Judah (Isaiah 1–5) 9

2. The Call of Isaiah (Isaiah 6–12) 18

3. Isaiah and Hezekiah (Isaiah 36–39) 30

4. Vision of a New Jerusalem (Isaiah 60–66) 39

INTRODUCTION

Byron Thomas

On numerous occasions during the forty-two years I have been in ministry, I have been approached by people of faith who initially stayed away from me because they had reservations about me, but they were concerned about what they had to share with me. Usually the conversation would begin with, "Pastor, you are going to think I'm crazy." Over the years, rather than tensing up for whatever "crazy" might sound like, I have learned to lean into these moments; for most of the time those who prefaced their conversation with these words did so because they were about to share the details of an experience they had with God—an experience of what is often referred to as "supernatural." Having no one else with whom they felt they could have this conversation, they approached their pastor. Being familiar with no other category in which they could place their experience, "crazy" was the only one they deemed most appropriate.

As I began to reflect on these experiences, it dawned on me that, on the one hand, the fact that those who approached me called their experience "crazy" was a demonstration of how far removed people of faith were from what would have been considered "ordinary" for those in the ancient world in general and more specifically to the writers of the Book of Isaiah. On the other hand, it was perhaps an example of the influence and impact of how the Age of Enlightenment and the world of fact and science had impacted our capacity to see and embrace what at one time had been widely accepted and understood by people of faith—that the non-factual world of the metaphysical had meaning, value, and relevance for our lives and times in which we live. I do not intend for this to be a criticism but simply an observation from a pastor who has more years behind me than I have in front of me.

The Book of Isaiah is an appropriate work for such reflection as it speaks to people who had experienced God's activity and revelation in the historical events of life through a variety of mediums that would have seemed perfectly normal. However, in our contemporary culture these same ways are often looked upon with suspicion and labeled "crazy." The opposite view would have been held by those of Isaiah's day. It would have been unimaginable for Isaiah to conceive of a world where visions, epiphanies, revelations, and dreams were not seen as normal and taken seriously. In fact, many would have believed that if you ignored these things, you did so at your own peril.

My approach to these sessions on Isaiah was largely pastoral. In a very real sense, my hope was to reframe the understanding of the experiences that people of faith have with God. Through identifying with Isaiah, believers might find a lens through which to gain a better understanding of their own "crazy" (supernatural) experiences as part of God's divine agency or ongoing work in the world. In a real sense, this is an effort to "normalize the abnormal" in a fact-based world that is the product of an Enlightenment world where science has largely shaped our worldview. This has ushered in an age that has even made people of faith question the sanity of their own metaphysical experiences and are often reticent to give witness to their own encounters with the Almighty.

Along with this, it is important to challenge the dualistic lens that often characterizes our approach to understanding Scripture and our interpretation of who God is and how our lives ought to be lived out before God. I proffer that the Book of Isaiah offers a more comprehensive as well as integrated understanding of the nature of God and divine agency. For example, Isaiah's experience before the throne of God in the sixth chapter demonstrates how being in the presence of the Sovereign God impacted Isaiah's capacity to accurately see who he was, as well as insight into the corporate identity of his fellow Jews and their corruption.

This is captured in the phrase "Woe is me! I am lost, for I am a man of unclean lips, and I live among a people of unclean lips; yet my eyes have seen the King, the Lord of hosts!" (Isaiah 6:5 NRSV). This comprehensive and integrated approach, as I see it, has significant implications for the relationship between what people of the Wesleyan tradition refer to as personal piety and social holiness. A dualistic approach fosters a perspective that personal piety and social holiness can exist separate and apart, thereby holding to the view that faith is "personal." On the other hand, this decoupling of personal piety from social holiness also results in a perspective that personal holiness is an unnecessary albatross, and that action, and in particular, social justice is the bellwether of legitimate faith.

The proffering of a more comprehensive, integrated view of Scripture over against a dualistic approach also has implications for worship in the Book of Isaiah. A dualistic understanding of worship tends to lean toward worship as something personal and private. A more corporate or integrated view of worship is rooted in the notion that worship is a generative experience. At the heart of worship is an "expectation" that what is done will ultimately enhance the possibility that those who are authentically engaged will have an encounter with God.

This encounter will lead to a deeper understanding of God, a more accurate understanding of ourselves, more authentic relationship with others, as well as insight into how sinister forces are at work in the systems that often govern our lives. However, and perhaps most importantly, this encounter will lead to greater faith, deeper living, agape love, and the type of commitment where one is willing to serve as an instrument of divine agency even if it may mean placing oneself in peril: "Then I heard the voice of the Lord saying, 'Whom shall I send, and who will go for us?' And I said, 'Here am I; send me!'" (Isaiah 6:8 NRSV).

Additionally, while I chose to take what I call a categorical approach to this work on Isaiah, this is more a reflection of our contemporary approach to the compartmentalization of things we seek to study and understand. While compartmentalized study is popular (literary criticism, historical criticism, biology, psychology, etc.), I am of the belief that this approach would have been foreign to Isaiah. Rather, his worldview would have been informed by a much more integrated approach where "right worship" had a direct impact as it related to issues of morality and ethics. While issues of personal piety and social justice are often seen as separate in our contemporary approach to Scripture, this would have not been possible in Isaiah's world and the biblical world at large.

As such, for Isaiah worship had less to do with the premium that is often placed on attendance, size, and social status than it had to do with drawing people into a closer and deeper relationship with God for the express purpose of being shaped by God and maintaining ongoing clarity regarding what it means to be God's people in the midst of constantly changing historical, social, and economic forces. How one understood and approached worship made a difference as to whether worship was something that was attended (I went to worship/church), or experienced (I expect to have an encounter with God). Attendance without the desire to have an encounter with God tended to lead to estrangement from God.

Finally, a consistent theme that runs through Isaiah is the naming of repeated opportunities God provides for God's people who were wayward in their worship and their behavior to return and enter into right relationship with God. There is a dogged determination to God's love such that God never gives up on those with whom God had been in covenant relationship: "And I will establish my covenant between me and you and your offspring after you throughout their generations, for an everlasting covenant, to be God to you and to your offspring after you" (Genesis 17:7 NRSV).

See now, the Lord, / the Lord Almighty, / is about to take from Jerusalem and Judah / both supply and support. (3:1)

1

PROPHECIES AGAINST JUDAH

Isaiah 1–5

DIMENSION ONE: WHAT DOES THE BIBLE SAY?

Answer these questions by reading Isaiah 1

1. How have the people's sins affected their relationship with God? (1:4) *they have rebelled against God – they dont know or understand God's ways*

2. What evidence of God's anger does the prophet cite? (1:7) *He calls the nation wounded from top of head to sole of foot — wounds + welts*

3. Why did anyone in the city of Jerusalem survive the invasion? (1:9) *If God had left no survivors, they'd have been like Sodom + Gomorrah*

4. Why is God offended by offerings? (1:13, 15) *What were your sacrifices like? meaningless assemblies / festivals of New Moon — appointed feast?*

5. What response does God desire? (1:16-17) *— spread out hands in prayer, hands are full of blood — Seek justice, encourage the oppressed / learn to do God*

9

NAVIGATING ISAIAH

6. What will God finally do for the people? (1:26).

Answer these questions by reading Isaiah 2

7. How are the contents of this chapter described? (2:1)

8. When will the prophet's expectations for the future be fulfilled? (2:2)

9. What are the expressions of time? (These expressions indicate a new topic or a new audience.) (2:2, 12, 20)

10. Why has God rejected the house of Jacob? (2:8, 18, 20)

11. What will God do to the proud? (2:11, 12)

Answer these questions by reading Isaiah 3

12. In what order are the country and capital city mentioned, compared to their order in 1:1 and 2:1? (3:1, 8)

13. Who is the speaker in verses 1-5? (3:4)

14. Who is the speaker in verses 6-8? (3:8)

PROPHECIES AGAINST JUDAH

15. What justification does the prophet give for the punishment of his society? (3:8-9)

16. What key words are repeated to give the chapter unity? (3:4, 6, 12, 14)

Answer these questions by reading Isaiah 4

17. What group of persons is discussed here? (4:1)

18. What introductory phrase is common to both verses 1 and 2? (4:2; see also 2:20; 3:18)

19. What does God want to happen? (4:3-4)

Answer these questions by reading Isaiah 5

20. What is the basic complaint concerning the vineyard? (5:2)

21. What action will the owner of the vineyard now take? (5:5-6)

22. What does the vineyard represent in this parable? (5:7)

23. What phrase is used to introduce the sections that follow? (5:8, 11, 18)

DIMENSION TWO: WHAT DOES THE BIBLE MEAN?

■ **Background.** Chapters 1–5 have a topical similarity, and may be called "Prophecies Against Judah." The prophet's speeches have been brought together to balance negative, judgmental sections with positive, hopeful ones. The positive speeches are 2:2-4 and 4:2-6. The entire section ends on a negative note (chap. 5). The collection appears to begin at 2:1. Chapter 1 was probably added as an introduction to the entire book when the "Prophecies Against Judah" were combined with other speeches.

■ **Isaiah 1.** The chapter has the following parts: introductory heading (v. 1), a word to survivors of a Judean national crisis (vv. 2-9), commentary on contemporary worship (vv. 10-20), and God's redemptive judgment (vv. 21-31). Within these sections, there may be other small divisions.

■ **Isaiah 1:2.** The appeal to the heavens and earth to hear the Lord's complaint against the people is a concept borrowed from international diplomacy and from the courts of law. Treaties and covenants between humans must be witnessed, so an agreement between God and people was said to be witnessed by "heavens" and "earth." Those witnesses are now called to testify to the rightness of God's cause. This analogy reveals the covenant background from which the prophet spoke.

■ **Isaiah 1:3-4.** What the people fail to know and understand is how gracious God has been to them in the past. Gratitude for God's generosity should now be translated into ethics. But their present activities make it clear how utterly estranged from that covenant concept the people have become (v. 4).

God's holiness will not allow the people to continue their sinful acts indefinitely. Such acts are in violation of a promise of fidelity the people made to the Holy One when they accepted the covenant.

PROPHECIES AGAINST JUDAH

- **Isaiah 1:7-9.** The prophet refers to an invasion of the country in the year 701 BC, when only the capital city and the Temple area (Zion) escaped destruction.
- **Isaiah 1:9.** The invasion is not presented solely as an instance of divine judgment for the people's sins. The narrow escape is attributed to God's continued and unmerited graciousness ("The Lord ... left us some survivors"). The realization of such graciousness ought to stimulate the people to change their priorities and repent.
- **Isaiah 1:10-20.** God is not pleased with rituals and sacrifice unless the worshiper also follows the laws that are part of the covenant. Note the expressions "meaningless offerings" and "worthless assemblies" (v. 13). The prophet is issuing, not a blanket rejection of the sacrificial system, but rejection of the rituals that are not accompanied by covenant obedience.
- **Isaiah 1:16.** The prophet refers to a ritual act that took place during the festival at which he was speaking. He suggests that the washing ought to be more than physical.
- **Isaiah 1:18-20.** God is still gracious. The future is still open, if the people will only respond in an appropriate way.
- **Isaiah 1:21-31.** The contrast between past and present in Jerusalem's religious life is dealt with here. The city, once faithful, has become degenerate, just as metal, mixed with impurities or water, becomes contaminated. God, compared to a metallurgist, will purge the society and restore to it its former condition.
- **Isaiah 1:29.** The worship of fertility deities was often carried out in sacred groves or gardens. Such activity has contributed to the people's estrangement from the Lord. Worship of these deities was thought to ensure the renewal of nature in the springtime. But in Israel's case, rather than a renewal, it will lead to withering destruction.
- **Isaiah 2.** This chapter has the following sections: an editorial introduction (v. 1), the goal of history (vv. 2-4), a personal word of exhortation (v. 5), three speeches

condemning pride and idolatry (vv. 6-11, 12-19, 20-21), and a final exhortation (v. 22).
- **Isaiah 2:6-21.** Three speeches that were delivered at different times and places seem to have been combined here (vv. 6-11, 12-19, 20-21). They may be read and appreciated independently, without searching for an overall progression of thought. Notice how certain themes or expressions tend to be repeated in each section. This repetition suggests a thematic collection.
- **Isaiah 3.** This chapter is made up of a series of speeches about the coming chaos in Judah and its causes. Note that some parts are poetry and some prose.
- **Isaiah 3:4.** The leaders of the country will be so thoroughly destroyed that only the inexperienced (boys and children) will be available to take their places.
- **Isaiah 3:16–4:1.** The women of the city are a new object of the prophet's criticism. This section seems to be made up of a series of once-independent criticisms. Prose and poetry are alternated. The section also contains introductory phrases such as "in that day." This section may have been joined to the larger context because of the theme of human pride (vv. 8, 16), and because women are mentioned in verse 12. The attack is not on dress itself, but on the preoccupation with dress to the exclusion of traditional religious values. This concern for clothing is merely a symptom of a deeper spiritual sickness.
- **Isaiah 4:5.** "Cloud of smoke by day and a glow of flaming fire by night" is an allusion to Exodus 13:21-22, where these objects symbolized God's presence during the desert journey. Those temporary signs will now be made permanent, an enduring sense of the divine presence. The same idea is conveyed by saying that the pavilion that accompanied the people in the desert (Exodus 40) will be a permanent fixture. The Book of Revelation uses a related image to reaffirm the divine presence: a "new Jerusalem" will descend from heaven (Revelation 21:1-4).

- **Isaiah 5.** This material may be divided into the parable of the vineyard (vv. 1-7), a series of "woe prophecies" condemning certain groups, and an outline of the resulting punishment (vv. 8-30).
- **Isaiah 5:1-7.** The parable has four stanzas, and the concluding one contains the interpretation (v. 7).
- **Isaiah 5:7.** The difference between the expected harvest and the wild grapes is translated into social terms by means of a pun that is lost in translation.
- **Isaiah 5:8-23.** The series of criticisms (introduced by "Woe to . . .") serves to illustrate the injustices in Judean society that may be compared with wild grapes.
- **Isaiah 5:8-10.** Accumulation of the real estate of others was frowned upon in Israel's sacred literature. This action fostered economic classes and inequality. It also was an arrogant assertion that humans were the absolute owners of land. By contrast, the ancient Israelites believed that land belonged to God. God graciously loaned it to the people (Leviticus 25). God's gift could not be taken away by someone else. The prophet says that the entire land will be taken away (the people will be exiled), and agriculture will fail as punishment for violating this ancient principle. It is especially appropriate that vineyards fail, in view of the previous parable of the vineyard. The prophet's disciples may have placed this woe (vv. 8-10) first in the sequence of "woes" for just this reason.
- **Isaiah 5:11-17.** The activities of the rich are not so wrong themselves. But they divert attention from traditional religious values. Just as appetites are insatiable, so are the forces of destruction ("Death"). Jerusalem will become a heap of ruins (v. 17), a theme in keeping with the parable in verses 1-7.
- **Isaiah 5:18-19.** Some people have become so callous in their disregard for the faith that they respond with arrogant mockery to anyone who reminds them of it. They say, in effect, "We challenge God to act, if God exists!"

■ **Isaiah 5:20-21.** These two woes denounce those who are clever enough to rationalize their base behavior until it appears justified ("those who call evil good"). In doing so, they deceive themselves, since they are clever only in their own eyes. In contrast, Israel's truly wise people assert that wisdom begins with reverence for the Lord (Proverbs 1:7).

DIMENSION THREE:
WHAT DOES THE BIBLE MEAN TO ME?

Isaiah 1:2-4—The Ingratitude of the Blessed

Israel's ancient traditions suggested that, although God had chosen and blessed the people, this need not have happened. Such actions were undeserved and should have generated a sense of gratitude in the people. This gratitude should be expressed in specific acts of obedience to God and in responsibility for others. Thus the prophets can accuse the people of more than the commission of wrong acts. The people are guilty of ingratitude and rebellion as well.

What gracious acts have been accorded the people of God throughout history? How is gratitude to God being expressed by the church (your church) today? How can the church better express gratitude to God? Can you cite instances of failure?

Isaiah 2:2-4—A Golden Age

The prophet has expressed the belief that the world need not remain as it is. Rather, he believes that God is working to bring about an ideal age "in the last days" (v. 2). Do you think the world has progressed toward the ideal since the time of Isaiah? Can you cite instances of success? Regressions? Is such a belief realistic? Do you believe it and strive toward it? What groups now are working toward that goal? Are they overtly religious groups?

Isaiah 5:1-7—God's Expectations of the Community

The prophet is struck by the vast gap between God's expectations for the people and the present reality. He believes that God has but one course of action if the situation is to be remedied. The people must be exiled to a foreign land. How can this episode be a model for understanding the present and future of the church? Is the church more obedient now than ancient Israel was? Is God more tolerant of the church's betrayals than of those in ancient Judah? Could the church be punished to the extreme that the ancient community was? What events today might be interpreted as God's judgment on the church? Could the church even be rejected? Could God start anew?

In the year that King Uzziah died, I saw the Lord, high and exalted, seated on a throne; and the train of his robe filled the temple. (6:1)

THE CALL OF ISAIAH

Isaiah 6–12

DIMENSION ONE: WHAT DOES THE BIBLE SAY?

Answer these questions by reading Isaiah 6

1. Where was the prophet when he had this religious experience? (6:1)

2. What was the prophet's response when he sensed the divine presence? (6:5)

3. How is God described? (6:1, 5)

4. What was the prophet commissioned to do? (6:10)

Answer these questions by reading Isaiah 7

5. What crisis set the stage for this chapter? (7:1, 2, 4)

THE CALL OF ISAIAH

6: What evidence is there that someone else besides Isaiah is the storyteller now? (7:3)

7. Who have King Ahaz's enemies threatened to put on the throne of Judah? (7:6)

Israel's Tabeel

8. Does the prophet think Ahaz's enemies will succeed? (7:7-8)

No

9. For whom is the sign intended? (7:14)

The House of David

10. How old will the boy be when Ahaz's enemies are defeated? (7:16)

Old enough to know right from wrong

11. What foreign power will take possession of Judah if the prophet's advice is not followed? (7:17)

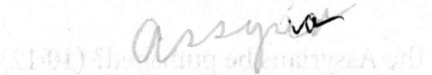

Assyria

Answer these questions by reading Isaiah 8

12. What foreign powers continue to threaten King Ahaz of Judah? (8:4)

Assyria

13. What does the prophet think will happen if the leaders of Judah refuse to listen? (8:7-8)

God's wrath

19

NAVIGATING ISAIAH

14. Was Isaiah a solitary individual, or did he have followers? (8:16)

15. Who do the people turn to for guidance in the crisis? (8:19)

Answer these questions by reading Isaiah 9

16. What parts of Israel have already fallen under Assyrian power? (9:1)

17. Where will the deliverer live, and over what will he rule? (9:7)

18. What phrase concludes each of several short speeches? (9:12, 17, 21; 10:4)

Answer these questions by reading Isaiah 10

19. For what sin will the Assyrians be punished? (10:12)

20. What does the prophet hope will finally happen? (10:21)

Answer these questions by reading Isaiah 11

21. With what image does this chapter begin? (11:1)

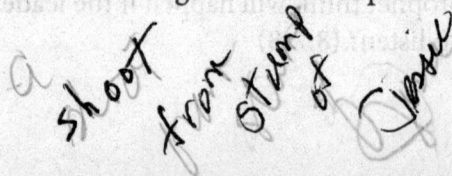

22. Rather than trust in his own power as Ahaz seems to have done, what will guide the new ruler? (11:2-3)

Answer this question by reading Isaiah 12

23. What is the people's attitude toward God now? (12:2)

DIMENSION TWO:
WHAT DOES THE BIBLE MEAN?

■ **Background.** Chapters 6–12 begin with Isaiah's summons to be a prophet. These chapters, written in prose, are concerned primarily with a major political crisis. The entire section may be described as "The Call of Isaiah."

■ **Isaiah 6:1.** King Uzziah's death signals the beginning of a time of uncertainty about the nation's future. The Assyrians had recently begun an aggressive expansion into Syria and Palestine, but King Uzziah was able to forge alliances that held them at bay. Isaiah, as he worships in the Temple, expresses his experience of God's presence and control in political terms. That is, he interprets it in a way that is relevant for the present.

■ **Isaiah 6:2.** The word *feet* is a common euphemism for genitals.

■ **Isaiah 6:3.** The repetition of words in the Hebrew language is a way of expressing emphasis. That "the whole earth is full of [God's] glory" means that all events are under divine control. Thus Uzziah's death need not be an occasion for despair.

■ **Isaiah 6:5.** Isaiah feels unworthy to exist. He feels God owes him nothing, not even life. His *lips* are mentioned, not because he has indulged in loose talk, but as a figure of speech where the part stands for the whole person.

21

- **Isaiah 6:6-7.** Isaiah can do nothing to remedy his status before God. Help can come only by an act of divine grace.
- **Isaiah 6:9-10.** The prophet's message, in accordance with God's wish, will provoke the people. Rather than repent, they will become even more stubborn and entrenched in their values and actions. This attitude will hasten the divine judgment.
- **Isaiah 6:11-13.** The nature and extent of the judgment now becomes clear. An invasion and destruction will occur at the hands of foreigners.
- **Isaiah 6:13.** Note that the prophet's commission, beginning at verse 9, ends one line short of the end of the chapter. The remaining line "But as the terebinth..." entirely changes the meaning of the passage. The prophet has used the word *stump* in a negative sense. Even those Judeans who survive the Assyrian attack will be destroyed, much as a stump is burned when shoots come up again. But the last line transforms the stump into a positive image. Life will survive in it, despite all destructive efforts. This line was probably added later. The prophet elsewhere has expressed a belief that a remnant would survive to form a new community (see the text note to Isaiah 7:3; see also 11:1). The "holy seed" is that surviving, righteous remnant.
- **Isaiah 7:2.** The rulers of Syria and Israel, fearful of an attack by the Assyrians, try to forge a new alliance to keep them at bay. *Ephraim*, the largest tribe in the Northern Kingdom, is sometimes used as a synonym for *Israel*.
- **Isaiah 7:3-6.** If Ahaz joins the alliance and it fails, Judah will be destroyed by the Assyrians. If he does not join it, the alliance will replace him with Tabeel, who favors their strategy. If he asks the Assyrians for help, he must become their vassal, and Judah's independence will be lost.
- **Isaiah 7:7-9.** Isaiah advises Ahaz to do nothing. The enemies will soon be defeated. The "it" that will not come to pass is the alliance and its plans.
- **Isaiah 7:8.** The word *for* obscures the meaning here. The Hebrew word can also be translated *that*. What is it that will

not endure as a threat to Ahaz: Damascus as the head of Syria (Aram) and Rezin as king of Damascus!
- **Isaiah 7:10-11.** These verses tell us that the king does not take Isaiah's advice. Ahaz explains that he will not test the Lord, as Isaiah has advised. As a matter of fact, however, the king may already have decided to ask the Assyrians to help, which he did (2 Kings 16:1-9).
- **Isaiah 7:14.** This sign has an entirely different purpose than the one the king has just refused to request. It will not determine foreign policy by convincing the king that Isaiah is giving him sound advice. Rather, it will serve to remind the king, once the crisis is over, that the prophet spoke the truth. Every time the king sees Immanuel, the king will be reminded that God was with the people in the crisis with the alliance, just as Isaiah had said! The child is likely the prophet's own son. He gave symbolic names to his other children during this same crisis (7:3; 8:3). The mother might be either the prophetess (8:3) or some other wife. The Hebrew word translated as *virgin*, is *almah*, which indicates a young woman.
- **Isaiah 7:15.** "Curds and honey" may mean that things will go well. Ahaz's policy will seem to have been a wise one.
- **Isaiah 7:17.** The prophet continues in a positive vein until the last clause. The days of curds and honey are a prelude to disaster. The Assyrians will be, not the saviors that Ahaz thought they were, but destroyers.
- **Isaiah 7:18-25.** This section contains a series of reflections on the future Assyrian presence in Judah. Each reflection begins with the traditional formula of introduction, "In that day..." (meaning "in days to come").
- **Isaiah 7:18-19.** The image of a fly or bee may have been used because those on whom they swarm are defenseless.
- **Isaiah 7:20.** Conquerors sometimes stripped captives and shaved them as a sign of dishonor (see comment on 6:2).
- **Isaiah 7:21.** The standard of living will be reduced to the lowest level. No one will have more than one or two animals. Only by that narrow margin will they escape starvation.

- **Isaiah 7:22.** This verse seems to promise abundance. Will those left in the land be fortunate compared to those slain or taken into exile?
- **Isaiah 8.** This chapter can be read in four sections. In verses 1-4, the prophet gives his son a symbolic name in anticipation of Judah's deliverance from the alliance. In verses 5-8, Isaiah's response to the king's failure to take his advice reflects the same tone as 7:10-17. Verses 9-10 reflect the optimistic period of 7:7-8 and 8:1-4. Verses 11-22 contain Isaiah's private reflections to his disciples after Ahaz rejects his advice.
- **Isaiah 8:3.** The "prophetess" (Isaiah's wife) may be the same woman as the young woman of 7:14. The events seem parallel.
- **Isaiah 8:6.** The waters of Shiloah are Jerusalem's water supply. They symbolize the life-giving advice that God has offered through the prophet.
- **Isaiah 8:7.** The Euphrates River marks a boundary of the Assyrian Empire. In these verses, the river symbolizes Assyria's power, as it does in 7:20. The Judeans, through their king, have chosen a raging and destructive river rather than a life-giving spring.
- **Isaiah 8:8.** The comforting name *Immanuel* (meaning "God is with us") is now used sarcastically.
- **Isaiah 8:11-15.** The prophet, disappointed that Ahaz has chosen to rely on the Assyrians rather than to trust the Lord, temporarily withdraws from public life. He now reflects on the situation in the presence of a small group of followers.
- **Isaiah 8:14-15.** The people, having rejected God's advice and offer of deliverance (8:5), will not find security. Having stumbled in their faith, they must suffer the consequences.
- **Isaiah 8:16-18.** Isaiah wants the people to know, in the difficult days ahead, that they had been offered an alternative. Isaiah's words and actions, including the names of his children, now serve as testimony to that fact. His disciples witness the fact that his warnings were delivered in advance, just as he claims.

THE CALL OF ISAIAH

- **Isaiah 8:19-22.** In a crisis, occult practices appeal to the people as a way to learn the future. Superstition cannot produce a new dawn for the people, and will only further the coming of exile.
- **Isaiah 9:1.** In response to the alliance that formed against him (see note on 7:2), the king of Assyria has attacked and added part of Israel to his empire. The conquered areas were Galilee (Zebulun and Naphtali), the coastal plain ("the Way of the Sea"), and the land beyond the Jordan. Isaiah believes their present gloom will end when God (the unexplained "he" in the passage) graciously acts on their behalf.
- **Isaiah 9:2.** In this section (vv. 1-7), Isaiah expects a new era beyond the period of Assyrian domination. Although the expected deliverance lies in the not-too-distant future, the prophet describes it in the past tense. Isaiah also believes the deliverer may already have been born (v. 6).
- **Isaiah 9:4.** The words *yoke*, *bar*, and *rod* all refer to the Assyrian oppressors. They will be expelled, just as the invading Midianites were cast out long ago (Judges 6:1–8:28).
- **Isaiah 9:6-7.** The era of restoration will take place under the leadership of a prince of the Davidic line. Isaiah's song may have been composed in celebration of that prince's birth and in anticipation of his accomplishments.
- **Isaiah 9:6.** Kings in the ancient Near East were often said to be godlike, and liked being addressed as "god." That a Judean king is described here in such terms is not surprising.
- **Isaiah 9:8-21.** We now return to the condemnation of the people for the pride and wickedness that characterized chapters 1–5.
- **Isaiah 9:8-9.** *Jacob* and *Israel* are equivalent terms in parallel poetic lines. Ephraim is the predominant tribe. Samaria is the capital city.
- **Isaiah 9:10.** The people, rather than heeding the prophet's warnings, become more determined to continue their traditional ways. This response illustrates the prophet's

25

commission in 6:10. Preaching to them will have a negative effect.

- **Isaiah 9:14.** This verse probably refers to the revolution that ended the reign of Ahab and Jezebel (2 Kings 9–10).
- **Isaiah 10.** This complex chapter may be divided into five sections: verses 1-4 continue the collection of paragraphs that began at 9:8, each ending with "his hand is still upraised." The next section is a commentary on the pride of the Assyrian conquerors (vv. 5-19). The third section is an expectation that the exiled Israelites will return (vv. 20-27). Verses 28-32 describe the Assyrian advance against Jerusalem in 701 BC. The final section deals with the consequences of the Assyrian attack (vv. 33-34).
- **Isaiah 10:1-4.** All previous means of communicating with the people of Judah have failed. They have not learned the lessons of history, and now divine judgment will fall (v. 4).
- **Isaiah 10:9.** Various places the Assyrian army has captured are cited, and they now approach Judah. Following their conquest of areas of Israel in 734–733 BC, they destroyed the capital city (Samaria) in 721. They exiled large elements of the population (2 Kings 17:1-6). Judah was spared because of King Ahaz's pro-Assyrian policy. However, his successor, King Hezekiah, tried to restore Judean independence from Assyria. Judah ultimately was invaded.
- **Isaiah 10:16.** This verse seems to reflect the fact that the Assyrian army withdrew from the siege of Jerusalem in 701 BC.
- **Isaiah 10:16-17.** Repeated use of the pronoun *he* can create confusion here: "his sturdy warriors," "his pomp," and "his thorns and his briers" refer to the king of Assyria. "Their Holy One" refers to God, here called the "Light of Israel."
- **Isaiah 10:22.** The purpose of the destruction that God has brought through the Assyrians is to produce a righteous remnant. God's judgment is ultimately redemptive.

THE CALL OF ISAIAH

- **Isaiah 10:24-27.** The tone of this section is so positive that it contrasts with much of Isaiah's previous message. The audience is addressed warmly, rather than as totally wicked (1:4). The Assyrians are presented as the enemies of God. They are not God's chosen instrument to punish a deserving Judah (5:26-30; 6:11-12; 7:18-25). This section was probably composed by Isaiah's disciples. They knew that the Assyrians withdrew in 701 BC. Perhaps they wanted to remember the prophet only in a positive and supportive light.
- **Isaiah 10:28-32.** The Assyrian advance (701 BC) is graphically described. "They," in verses 28-29, are the forces of Sennacherib, king of Assyria.
- **Isaiah 10:33-34.** Presumably, these verses describe the results of the Assyrian advance outlined in 10:28-32. Lebanon (Syria and Palestine) and Judah will be cut down by the invading Assyrians as easily as foresters cut down trees.
- **Isaiah 11.** Chapter 11 deals with the expectation of a new era under the leadership of a righteous member of the royal house, and the return of the people from their exile (vv. 10-16).
- **Isaiah 11:1.** Jesse was the father of David, so the verse is referring to the traditional royal family. Only when the tree is cut down can a new, vigorous shoot come forth.
- **Isaiah 11:2-5.** This ruler will rely on God rather than on his own schemes. He will be what God wanted human leadership to be when the monarchy was first instituted.
- **Isaiah 11:6-9.** The recovery of the harmonious world God intended at creation is described in poetic language.
- **Isaiah 12.** This chapter is a song of praise. The congregation confesses that God's judgment has been merited and was ultimately redemptive.

NAVIGATING ISAIAH

DIMENSION THREE:
WHAT DOES THE BIBLE MEAN TO ME?

Isaiah 6:9-13—How Is Success to Be Measured?

Has the prophet been commissioned by God to be a failure? What is it, positively, that he is to try to accomplish? Is the prophetic task different from the ministerial task today? How is the prophet's strange mission similar to a minister's task today? Which ministers are successful in the public mind? Why?

Isaiah 7:14—The Old Testament in the New

This verse is cited in the New Testament in connection with the birth of Jesus (Matthew 1:23). Specifically, what use does Matthew make of Isaiah 7:14? Which of the following do you think is most nearly correct? (1) What Isaiah meant is clarified by the New Testament. Matthew 1:23 is the inspired translation of the prophet. The prophet has been able to see far into the future and predict the birth of Jesus. (2) What Isaiah meant is clarified by reading his words in their literary and historical context. He referred to a child in his own time, and Matthew misunderstood him. (3) Matthew is drawing a parallel, not predicting. Just as God gave a sign then—that God is with us—God gives a sign now. Use of the word *fulfill* (Matthew 1:22) need not mean "to make a prediction come true."

Isaiah 8:19-20—The Prophet and Mediums

When, in times of crisis in the Bible, have people turned to wizards and mediums to learn about the future? Do you know, or know of, persons who claim to have the ability to contact the dead? What is your opinion of this practice? What does the prophet seem to regard as the only legitimate

28

source of knowledge of the supernatural? Which of the following do you think is more nearly correct? (1) The Bible means that people can actually do such things, but the faithful should not participate in them. (2) The Bible merely describes people who claim to do such things. It does not necessarily acknowledge that they are successful.

Isaiah 10:33–11:1—How to Effect a Change of Heart

The prophet calls for repentance—a genuine, enduring change of heart or of priorities. What are some shallow motives for change, which might have been at work until God took drastic measures? When have you repented out of fear, or because it appeared to be the smart thing to do under the circumstances? Did that repentance "stick" to effect true change, or did you revert to comfortable behavior when the circumstances changed? Do persons, or even institutions, usually reform spontaneously? Is some pressure necessary to bring about change? Are God's judgment and grace opposite sides of God, or are they really "two sides of the same coin"? When have you seen both these elements at work at the same time?

The time will surely come when everything in your palace, and all that your predecessors have stored up until this day, will be carried off to Babylon. (39:6)

3

1988 page

ISAIAH AND HEZEKIAH

Isaiah 36-39

DIMENSION ONE:
WHAT DOES THE BIBLE SAY?

Answer these questions by reading Isaiah 36

1. In what way does this chapter begin differently from all of the previous ones? (36:1)

in 14th yr of K, Hezekiah's reign + Sennacherib King of Syria ... captured all fortified cities of Judah

2. Why has the king of Assyria sent his army against Judah? (36:5)

you do not have strategy, military strength you speak w/ empty words ... On Whom do you depend?

3. What foreign power have the Judeans expected to come to their aid? (36:6)

Egyptians - Pharaoh - a "splintere reed or staff"

4. What deity has summoned the Assyrian army into Judah, according to the Assyrian general? (36:10)

the Lord our God - the one Hezekial removes - saying Worship before this altar

5. Why has the Lord summoned the Assyrians? (36:7)

Says Lord himself told me (King of Assyria to march vs. "this country"

30

1947

ISAIAH AND HEZEKIAH

Answer these questions by reading Isaiah 37

6. What does Hezekiah hope for? (37:4)

maybe Lord God will hear field commander + will rebuke him - rebuke him - leaving a

7. How have the Assyrian plans offended the Lord? (37:29) remnant

they have mocked His power

8. What does the prophet expect? (37:35)

God will defend the city + David

Answer these questions by reading Isaiah 38

9. What is the basis of Hezekiah's appeal for a longer life? (38:3)

his faithful + wholehearted - has done good

10. What is the cause of the king's illness? (38:17) — a boil

God's hand released him from agony — God sees his king seeking his own

11. What can't the dead do? (38:18-19)

they cannot hope for God's faithfulness — only the living can praise you —

Answer these questions by reading Isaiah 39

12. What enemy nation now emerges? (39:1)

Babylon

13. What was Hezekiah's attitude toward this potential ally against Assyria? (39:2)

he bragged showed Babylonian emissaries all of his wealth

14. What future does the prophet expect at the hands of the Babylonians? (39:6-7)

all riches will be carried off — you will become eunuchs in palace of Babylon — Hezekiah believes prosper as long as he lives

DIMENSION TWO: WHAT DOES THE BIBLE MEAN?

■ **Background.** Chapters 36–39 of Isaiah are largely prose, whereas what comes before and after them is almost entirely poetry. When such change occurs, the modern interpreter should be aware of the possibility of a new audience, a new historical situation, and possibly a new speaker.

In terms of theme, chapters 36–38 stress that Jerusalem is secure from conquest by the Assyrians. You should remember that such confidence conflicts with Isaiah's expectation that this enemy would indeed destroy the city (Isaiah 5:1-7; 6:11-13; 7:18-25; 30:12-14). However, other passages in the book express confidence in the city's security, such as 16:4-7; 30:29-33; 31:8-9. Since those optimistic passages seem to reflect the opinion of the prophet's disciples, we may wonder whether chapters 36–38 are not from a later period as well. This idea would help to account for the fact that Isaiah does not speak in the first person. His actions and words are described in the third person: "Isaiah ... sent" (37:21), "Isaiah ... went" (38:1), and "Isaiah said" (39:5).

With the aid of notes in your Bible, you will discover that Isaiah 36–39 is parallel to 2 Kings 18:13–20:19. In fact, the wording is identical from 2 Kings 18:19 onward. Why this repetition? Was one passage copied from the other? If so, in which book did the passage originate? Read both sections in their contexts. You will note that the account in Second Kings is an essential part of the storyline. Deleting the passage in Second Kings leaves a noticeable gap. By contrast, the account may be dropped from Isaiah without leaving a trace. So the passage probably has been borrowed from Second Kings, perhaps by the prophet's disciples. The purpose would have been to give a more complete report of Isaiah's ministry; all the stories of Isaiah in a single collection. Why locate them here after chapter 35; perhaps

ISAIAH AND HEZEKIAH

because the previous collection of prophecies, chapters 28–35, stress the security of Jerusalem. These stories will provide a continuity of theme.

The event that the passage describes is one already familiar to readers of the Book of Isaiah: the Assyrian invasion of 701 BC (see the note to Isaiah 22:1-2). King Hezekiah of Judah has decided not to honor his alliance with Assyria. The Assyrians have arrived to force his compliance (see the notes to Isaiah 20:1-2; 31:1-3). Later, the Assyrians withdraw. This move seems to have caught the prophet by surprise (Isaiah 22). But he interprets the withdrawal as a sign of God's graciousness (Isaiah 1:9).

The portrait just sketched, from genuine Isaiah prophecies, differs at points from the account in chapters 36–37.

- **Isaiah 36–37.** These two chapters are meant to be read as a continuous story. However, as you read it, you may notice that more than one account has been combined. Look for repetitions and differing points of view.
- **Isaiah 36:1.** No other chapter in Isaiah begins by dating the year of the king's reign. By contrast, narratives often begin this way in the books of Kings (see, for example, 1 Kings 15:1; 2 Kings 3:1; 12:1; 13:1). This introduction suggests that the story has been borrowed from Kings.
- **Isaiah 36:2.** The word *Rabshaketh* in the NRSV refers to an office rather than a name. In the NIV, it is translated as "field commander."
- **Isaiah 36:6.** For previous mention of Judah's reliance on Egypt as an ally against Assyria, see Isaiah 20:5-6; 30:2; 31:1-3.
- **Isaiah 36:7.** Hezekiah, in an effort to reform Judean worship, had closed many traditional sanctuaries. He has encouraged the people to come to Jerusalem instead, "this altar" (see 2 Kings 18:1-6). This effort probably provoked opposition from local priests; some of them may have thought that the king should be punished (just as the Assyrian general proposes).

NAVIGATING ISAIAH

■ **Isaiah 36:10.** The Assyrian general proposes that he is the Lord's agent. He has been sent to punish Judah. Judah has not only destroyed traditional sanctuaries (v. 7), but has broken its alliance with Assyria. Such alliances involved the taking of oaths in God's name. When oaths are broken, one has angered the deity by swearing falsely.

■ **Isaiah 36:11.** Aramaic was the language of international diplomacy at the time.

■ **Isaiah 37:3.** The country's dangerous situation is illustrated by an analogy. The situation is like a woman who develops complications during childbirth and is in extreme danger.

■ **Isaiah 37:22-32.** The *you* of verses 22-39 is the king of Assyria. The *you* of verse 30 is Hezekiah. The *I* of verses 24-25 is the king of Assyria. The *I* of verse 26 is the Lord.

■ **Isaiah 37:26.** The king of Assyria should not boast about his conquests, as if they resulted from his own initiative and ability. In fact, the Lord is using him in accordance with previous divine plans.

■ **Isaiah 38.** Although the chapter has a single theme (Hezekiah's sickness), it has the following parts, possibly of separate origin: (1) a prose account of the king's affliction and of God's promise (vv. 1-8); (2) a poetic prayer of thanksgiving, perhaps a traditional prayer that is now placed in the mouth of the king (vv. 10-20); and (3) details of the story that apparently were accidentally left out (vv. 21-22).

■ **Isaiah 38:8.** Use of the word *dial* in the NRSV is an interpretation of the translator. The NIV translates the word more literally as *stairway*.

■ **Isaiah 38:12-13.** The words *you* and *he* refer to God, presumed to be the ultimate source of the king's suffering.

■ **Isaiah 38:16.** This verse is unclear in the context. At such points, compare translations, and if possible, consult a good commentary. The CEV translates the line, "Your words and your deeds bring life to everyone, / including me. / Please make me healthy and strong again."

- **Isaiah 38:20.** This verse is out of place; it looks forward to the healing that verses 17-19 have already announced as accomplished.
- **Isaiah 38:21-22.** These verses, in prose, belong back in the prose narrative (vv. 1-8). They seem to be an afterthought, necessary to explain the prose account. How did God heal the king (v. 6)? What prompted the prophet to offer the king a sign (v. 7)? In actuality, these verses are not afterthoughts, but verses that have been accidentally lost from the prose narrative. This fact can be verified by reading the parallel account at 2 Kings 20:7-8.
- **Isaiah 39:1.** The Babylonian ruler, himself in rebellion against the Assyrians, is seeking an ally in the king of Judah. His gift, therefore, is politically motivated.
- **Isaiah 39:5-7.** The passage attempts to explain why the Babylonians destroyed the holy city. Earlier, Hezekiah had shown them the wealth of the city and the Temple. Presumably, this destruction was a violation of the sanctity of the place (an offense to God). It may have incited greed that was not soon to be forgotten.

DIMENSION THREE:
WHAT DOES THE BIBLE MEAN TO ME?

Isaiah 36–39—Historical Correctness and Faith

Chapters 36–39 of Isaiah present new illustrations of a problem that have arisen previously. Is the text historically correct in its details? For example, could the Assyrians have withdrawn from Jerusalem because Hezekiah promised to pay the tribute they had come to collect? Their own account suggests that this was the case. And, some support may be found in 2 Kings 18:13-16, deleted from the version in Isaiah. Would the Assyrian king withdraw and relinquish what was due, merely because of a rumor (Isaiah 37:7)? How can we explain such a monumental loss as 185,000 soldiers within a single night?

35

The problem now is compounded because of conflicting accounts of what happened. For example, did the Assyrians withdraw before siege work could even begin (Isaiah 37:33-35)? Or did they, in fact, besiege the city strenuously and for some time? (Isaiah 1:9; 29:1-3).

How important is it to you that various accounts of an event are in total agreement? Is agreement among biblical accounts a matter of faith to you? Do you think these considerations were important to those who told the biblical stories or to those who heard them? Or did they have a different concern? If so, what was their concern? How does (or can) this account inform our faith if we treat it as a record of God's activities and intentions toward us rather than focusing on its historical accuracy in all details?

Isaiah 37—Reinterpretation Within Scripture

When the story of Jerusalem's survival from Assyrian conquest was written, several emphases of the prophet Isaiah were preserved. He had urged the monarch and the citizens of the place to believe in the possibility of deliverance (7:7-9). He had asked them to trust in God rather than in foreign alliances (30:15). He had condemned the arrogance of the Assyrians whom God had summoned to punish the unfaithful Judeans (10:5-19). In these cases, the great prophet would have been pleased that his emphases remained alive in the thought of succeeding generations. But he might have been a bit surprised that new conclusions were reached by those who came after him, and that some of those conclusions were now being proposed as his own.

The punishment of the Assyrians, which Isaiah had expected to happen after they conquered Jerusalem (10:5-19), is now proposed as his expectation on them even before they could approach Jerusalem (37:33-35). The faith that he had proclaimed as a precondition of deliverance (7:9) is now replaced by an assurance of deliverance with no preconditions (37:5-7). Israel is delivered for the sake of David (37:35). In any case, this writing suggests that faithlessness and a failure to trust God are corrected by some kind of punishment. What do you think about the effectiveness of sanctions or punishments in gaining better results? What other methods may work as well? In what ways does genuine transformation take place?

Isaiah 36–37—Is Jerusalem Secure?

Those who composed the story of Jerusalem's deliverance, as we now have it in chapters 36–37, wanted to move the hearer beyond concerns for military tactics and the economy to matters of faith in God. The ultimate word about the future does not rest with human oppressors, such as Sennacherib of Assyria or any of his successors. Human rulers of the people of God should not forget God's sovereignty. They should be like the pious and trusting Hezekiah, and not like his predecessors. But beyond these generalities, deciding how the composers intended the story to be heard is difficult.

Did they mean to imply that Jerusalem was forever secure from foreign invasion? Some persons in Judah were confident of that (2 Samuel 7:4-16; Jeremiah 7:1-4; 26:7-11; Psalms 89:1-4; 132:11-18). Such a conclusion can be derived from Isaiah 36–37 only by analogy, however: Just as God delivered the sacred city from Sennacherib, so we trust that God will deliver it from the Assyrians at present.

Those who read the corresponding chapters in Second Kings would have been less likely to make such an analogy. There, the history of Judah continues beyond the reign of Hezekiah, and he is succeeded by the evil King Manasseh. The security of the city erodes, and prophets announce its impending destruction (2 Kings 21:10-15). We should not be surprised, therefore, that the later Babylonians succeeded in doing what the Assyrians could not. Does the story in Kings suggest that this destruction would not have

NAVIGATING ISAIAH

happened had the rulers been as willing to trust God as had Hezekiah?

Which of the following do you think is the more appropriate reaction? (1) These chapters contain an interesting, and perhaps valid, interpretation of the Assyrian invasion. But that single event is long past, and we do not live in Jerusalem. The passage promises no security for any other spot and time. We may, however, learn something about God's control of history, and admire the faith of Hezekiah. (2) Although we do not live in Jerusalem, we can learn something about the source of security that is beyond all others. We ought to trust in God, rather than in military weapons and political alliances. If we do so, we will be secure. (3) No amount of faith, or trust in God, is an absolute guarantee of political security for any group. However, we can learn something from this passage about God's control of history. If we lose our security, that too is within God's providence. We must try to learn from that experience, and start anew.

*See, I will create new heavens and a new earth. /
The former things will not be remembered. (65:17)*

4

VISION OF A NEW JERUSALEM

Isaiah 60–66

DIMENSION ONE: WHAT DOES THE BIBLE SAY?

Answer these questions by reading Isaiah 60

1. Who does this chapter address? (60:10-11, 14)

2. What are the people who were in exile doing? (60:4)

3. How does the prophet describe the restored community? (60:11, 17, 21)

Answer these questions by reading Isaiah 61

4. Has the restoration of the city begun yet? (61:4)

5. What will be the attitude of foreigners toward the community? (61:6)

NAVIGATING ISAIAH

6. What is the response of the community to this proposed new status? (61:10)

Answer this question by reading Isaiah 62

7. What is the new relationship between God and the people compared to? (62:4-5)

Answer these questions by reading Isaiah 63

8. What event from the past is the prophet citing? (63:11-12)

9. What suggests that a group within the community is praying, rather than the entire group? (63:16)

10. What tragedy has befallen the sanctuary? (63:18)

Answer these questions by reading Isaiah 64

11. To what do the speakers attribute their present misfortunes? (64:5-6)

12. What does the speaker ask for? (64:8-9)

Answer these questions by reading Isaiah 65

13. How did Judah respond to God's presence? (65:1-2)

VISION OF A NEW JERUSALEM

14. Who is God going to save? (65:8-9)

15. Although the prophet speaks of new heavens and a new earth, what is his real concern? (65:17-18)

pandemic hatred vs. Asians "somebody to hate"
racism it need to find sheets modes

Answer these questions by reading Isaiah 66

16. What evidence is there of divisiveness within the community? (66:5)

17. How have skeptics described the half-finished restoration of Jerusalem? (66:9)

18. How will God treat Jerusalem? (66:12-13)

19. Why are messengers sent to the nations? (66:19)

God is in the midst of historical events of one day — find the

DIMENSION TWO:
WHAT DOES THE BIBLE MEAN?

God promises standing for recog. of people who long

■ **Background.** Chapters 56–66 are among the most *God* controversial and difficult chapters in the entire Book of Isaiah. Modern interpreters disagree about how many authors there are, how many units of speech there are, and about the range of dates involved (suggestions range from the late sixth to the early second centuries BC).

■ **Isaiah 60–62.** These chapters, continuing the enthusiasm and optimism that characterized chapters 40–55, are sometimes attributed to the second Isaiah. Usually they are thought to be the earliest speeches of the third Isaiah. They

God has made us for himself

differ only slightly from the speeches of Second Isaiah. They differ more from the chapters that follow them.

- **Isaiah 60.** God is the speaker throughout, even when we see references in the third person (the word *his* in v. 2). Note the first-person references in verses 7, 10, 15, 17, and especially 22. (This sets the chapter apart from chap. 61, where the prophet speaks of himself). The audience seems to be in Jerusalem and not in Babylonia, as they were in chapters 40–55.
- **Isaiah 60:19-20.** The writer of Revelation made use of these ideas at 21:3 and 22:5.
- **Isaiah 61:1-11.** In verses 1-3, the prophet states his self-understanding. Verses 4-9 reveal what God's activity will mean for the audience. The congregation then responds to God's message (vv. 10-11).
- **Isaiah 61:3.** Although this speech may have been delivered soon after the return of the exiles (539 BC), despair already has begun. The task of restoration and the lack of resources are overwhelming. The expression "in Zion" fixes the prophet's location.
- **Isaiah 61:11.** Lest the audience expect overnight results, the prophet compares restoration to the growth of nature. Results are sure, but the process has its own schedule.
- **Isaiah 62.** The prophet's insistent tone may suggest that time has passed since his announcements in chapters 60–61.
- **Isaiah 62:2.** A new name signals a new beginning, as when Jacob's name is changed to Israel (Genesis 35:10). The new names are given in verse 4.
- **Isaiah 62:4.** *Deserted* was used to describe the community previously (54:6; 60:15; see also Jeremiah 4:29). *Desolate* was also a description of Judah (1:7; 6:11; Jeremiah 4:27; 6:8). The analogy of marriage and divorce to describe God's relationship to the people is common in the prophets (50:1; 54:5).
- **Isaiah 62:8.** These verses reverse the curse that prophets sometimes announced (Micah 6:15).
- **Isaiah 62:10-12.** The speaker now imitates the style and vocabulary of the second Isaiah at 40:3-4, 9-10.

VISION OF A NEW JERUSALEM

- **Isaiah 63:1-6.** The question "Who is this coming?" is one a sentry would ask. The word *Edom* is probably used here as a symbol for all enemies of the community.
- **Isaiah 63:7–64:12.** Before addressing God about the problems of the present at verse 15, the speaker recites evidence of God's willingness to act in the past (63:7-14). This recitation of the past gives hope in the present. Following the plea for help is a confession of sin (64:5-7), an expression of confidence (64:8), and a resumption of the plea (64:9-12).
- **Isaiah 63:7-14.** This section of the prayer (whether recited by the prophet or the community is not clear) is similar to Psalm 44. It may be a familiar piece of liturgy rather than a composition by the prophet.
- **Isaiah 63:10.** This verse apparently refers to the Exile.
- **Isaiah 63:16.** The expression "though Abraham does not know us / or Israel acknowledge us" is obscure. Some interpreters think the prophet's followers lament that the priestly leaders of Judah do not share their point of view. The expressions may mean that the community, in its struggles, no longer seems to share in the promises made to Abraham and Israel (Jacob). The "fathers" of the community, here treated as if they are still present, do not favor the community.
- **Isaiah 63:18.** Does this verse refer to the destruction of the Temple in 587 BC at the hands of the Babylonians? Or does it refer to a brief period in the immediate past when the prophet's community had control of liturgical leadership? This period ended when the Zadokite/Aaronite priests came to power.
- **Isaiah 64:1.** The prophet here refers to stories of God's past appearances (Exodus 19:16-18; Psalm 18:7-9).
- **Isaiah 64:11.** The reference to the burned Temple as if it were a recent event has caused some interpreters to suggest that 63:7–64:12 was composed by Judeans who remained behind when the exiles were taken away. If so, the passage would be earlier than the time of the third Isaiah.

43

- **Isaiah 65:1-25.** This chapter illustrates well how the shape of prophetic preaching has changed. The message of the preexilic prophets was almost entirely negative. The message of the exilic Second Isaiah was almost entirely positive in accordance with the needs of the situation. Now we find a mixture of doom and salvation.

  The Judeans no longer agree in their attitude toward God. Some are responsive, some are not. It would do no good to condemn the whole for the sake of the wicked. Such an approach would not now be effective. Moreover, the second Isaiah had renounced such an approach in God's name (54:7-10). So, following a word of condemnation for some (65:1-7) is a statement of distinction (v. 8), then a mixture of positive and negative prophecies (vv. 9-16). Finally, the prophet shifts from moral comparisons to comparing the present and the future (vv. 17-25).
- **Isaiah 65:4.** Consulting the spirits of the dead about the future was well known in the ancient Near East (1 Samuel 28).
- **Isaiah 65:11.** *Fortune* and *Destiny* are titles of deities.
- **Isaiah 65:17-25.** This powerful vision of a renewed world is made up of quotations and allusions to earlier sayings in the Book of Isaiah.
- **Isaiah 65:1-19.** The idea here is picked up from 35:10; 51:11. The idea will, in turn, inspire the author of Revelation 21:1-4.
- **Isaiah 65:25.** This verse is a close paraphrase of 11:6-9.
- **Isaiah 66:1-14.** This chapter is one of the most difficult in Isaiah in terms of the relationship of its various topics. Has it as many as seven separate units or as few as one? The meaning changes according to how verses are grouped together.
- **Isaiah 66:1-2.** (1) Is this speech against temple building as such? (2) Does it oppose only the present plans, which were different from the Temple that was destroyed? (3) Does the speech oppose only the claim that God's blessing depends on completion of the Temple (as the contemporary prophet

Haggai proclaimed in 2:18-19)? (4) Is this speech traditional praise of God as one whose glory no temple can contain (as in 1 Kings 8:27)? Verse 2b (if it is an original continuation of verses 1-2a) suggests the third of these options.

■ **Isaiah 66:3-4.** The grammar of verse 3a is obscure. Perhaps a comparison is being made, stating that all sacrificial acts are forbidden (see option 1 above). This verse may be condemning both legitimate and illegitimate cultic acts. The CEV uses the translation, "You sacrifice oxen to me, / and you commit murder." The latter possibility is more likely, in view of criticism of strange cultic practices in 65:3-5 and 66:17 (all three verses refer to pigs as sacrificial animals).

■ **Isaiah 66:5.** This verse could be an independent pronouncement. Or it could continue a speech that began in verse 1, so that "you who tremble at his word" would refer to the same groups as does verse 2 ("tremble at my word"). The prophet's own community has been hated and cast out by the predominant priestly leadership. This interpretation would mean that those who do the terrible things in verse 3 are not merely individuals here and there, but the official leadership in the Temple. Their activities may be described in exaggerated terms. Even if the verse is an independent statement, the community is deeply divided over religious matters, and the prophet's point of view is not the official one.

■ **Isaiah 66:18-23.** The divisiveness within the community that chapters 63–66 have alluded to is now balanced with a vision of a united community. This passage is similar in spirit to chapters 60–62, and to the ideas of the second Isaiah. In fact, it may have been intended to return to a theme that began the book: the "all the nations" will come "to my holy mountain" (66:20), just as in 2:2, "all the nations will stream to it."

■ **Isaiah 66:22-23.** The permanence of the new situation is stressed for those who might wonder if the problems of the past could return. (The same point was made by the second Isaiah at 54:9-10; 51:6).

NAVIGATING ISAIAH

■ **Isaiah 66:24.** The permanence of the salvation that verses 22-23 describe is not paralleled by a statement of the permanent demise of human rebelliousness. The memory of the terrible cost of human pride will not be forgotten. The prophet puts this graphically; the corpses will be a perpetual reminder. This verse is not a reference to punishment in hell, which is a later concept.

DIMENSION THREE: WHAT DOES THE BIBLE MEAN TO ME?

Isaiah 65:25—The Apocalyptic Outlook

The prophet was troubled by tensions in the community and opposition by neighbors. He could not find hope in the framework of ordinary history. The optimism of chapters 60-62 fades. The appeal to the community to obey and reform itself is replaced by announcements of destruction. An appeal is made for a purge of the world that will produce an unending utopia. This point of view, arising from the situation of the third Isaiah, contrasts with the optimism we find in the second Isaiah.

Compare the outlook of the third Isaiah with that of the first Isaiah (see esp. chaps. 1-39). Consider, for example, the nearly identical sayings that are found at 65:25 and 11:6-9. How do their expectations for the future differ? What accounts for that difference? Why might each prophet have refused to adopt the stance of the other? When is an apocalyptic stance helpful to the community and faithful to God? What about apocalyptic announcements in the present? When are these announcements helpful? When are they harmful?

46

Isaiah 65:1-7—What Is God Really Like?

Christians will occasionally portray the God of ancient Israel and the Old Testament as aloof and judgmental. The God of Jesus is portrayed as near, forgiving, and loving. Discuss this attitude in light of Isaiah 65:1-7.

Isaiah 65:17-25—Utopia

The ideal future as outlined in 65:17-25 differs from later portraits of the age to come. Compare these verses with Revelation 21:1-4, and note any differences. Something the writer of Revelation regards as an absolute evil, to be abolished forever, the third Isaiah does not regard as a problem.

Why do you think death came to be seen as a theological problem? Why was it not a matter of great concern to the third Isaiah or any of his predecessors in the Old Testament? What are your own personal feelings about mortality?

Sara & David - fighting cancer
David's cousin Rick (death)
Praise - Phyllis's father (95)
Betsy Ovoaere - on pillow - wife -
  thanks Phyllis -
Jean in surgery Wed.